# Life on Location

To/ Violet

Enjoy the many locations you travel to.

With love

Sheila

xx

First published 2023



Published under licence by Brown Dog Books and
The Self-Publishing Partnership Ltd, 10b Greenway Farm, Bath Rd,
Wick, nr. Bath BS30 5RL

www.selfpublishingpartnership.co.uk

ISBN printed book: 978-1-83952-659-6

Cover design by Andrew Prescott
Internal design by Andrew Easton
Illustrated by Emma Hopkins

Printed and bound in the UK

This book is printed on FSC® certified paper

FSC
www.fsc.org
MIX
Paper | Supporting responsible forestry
FSC® C013604

# Life on Location

## A collection of poems from life's journey


Sheila Hopkins

Illustrated by Hop

(aka Emma Hopkins)



BROWN DOG BOOKS

# Poet's Voice

If you were expecting a poetry book about being on a film set, I'm afraid this is not it. I've called this book 'Life on Location' because I've found that quite often my poetry is influenced by the place or phase of life I'm in. Life is a journey and poems happen in the places we find ourselves.

A poem captures the moment - an incident, an encounter, an exhilarated feeling held in a few words. By pressing the pause button just long enough, a fragment of life is put on a page. A poem can be about anything. Life condensed - fewer words than prose - expressing the minute detail of a scene observed - the smell of coffee, the dampness of the dew, the spiralling of a leaf dangling from a strand of spider's web; the intensity of a feeling; the humour of life.

I first started writing poetry when I was working as an English teacher nearly forty years ago. Since then, my writing has been a bit sporadic. I'll find that I write lots of poems all at once and then none for ages. There isn't any reason why I start writing again, but sometimes a poem just sneaks up on me. I'll start with an idea and as I sit to write, the words begin to flow. I'm always happiest with the poems that make people laugh, but I realise that I probably write more of the reflective ones these days. I really enjoy reading my poetry out loud and I'm grateful to friends and family who've patiently and encouragingly listened to my readings. The spoken word has more impact so I'm sorry if they don't seem quite the same, sitting flat on the page. You could try reading them aloud and playing with the rhythm of the words until the poem comes alive for you. Perhaps I'll have the opportunity to read them to you myself one day.

The poems have been illustrated by Hop (aka Emma Hopkins.) Thanks, Emma.

Thanks to my family, David, Emma, Joel and Tom, and my friends, Angela, Ray, and Kara for all your support and encouragement.

*Sheila Hopkins*

(aka Hop's mum, Joel's mum, Tom's mum and David's wife.)

## A note from the illustrator

It has been a delight and an amazing, creative adventure to illustrate my mum's poems. I am so proud of her for taking the plunge to finally publish her poetry. I have been moved to tears, laughed out loud and walked down paths of remembering. I hope you relish her way with words as I have. I am grateful and blessed to call such a wonderful, generous, shiny human my mum. Hop :)

# List of Poems

London

## POWER CUT

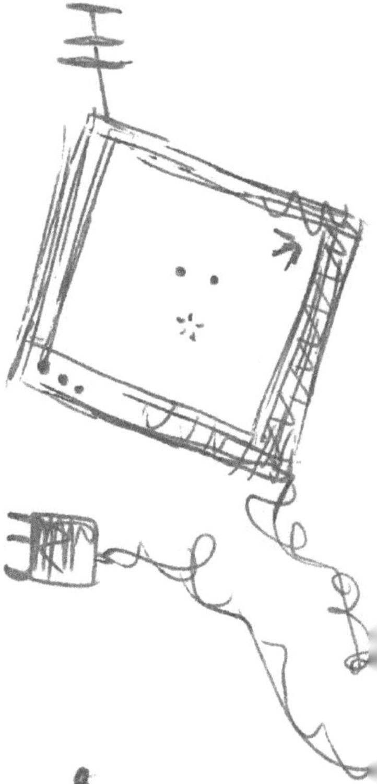

Dusky, wintery, afternoon chill
Slithers along
Unlit, car-lined streets.
No welcoming glow issues forth
From darkened doorways.

Living room curtains
Drawn against the night
Shield darkness from darkness.
No warm light beckons you home.
Here and there
A candle flickers.

Televisions are silenced
Radios and hi-fi systems
Remain mute.
In a hundred kitchens,
Where suppers should be sizzling,
Bubbling, spluttering,
The smells of cooking disperse
As half-cooked food
Stands ruined.

No hairdryers whirr,
No kettles hum,

London

No fridges murmur.
Machinery is silenced.

And we,
Electricity-reliant citizens,
Flounder helplessly,
Hungry and cold,
Wondering how far we must go
To find the nearest take-away
Still 'frying tonight'!

## WASHING DAY NIGHTMARE

Oh, English weather,
How unpredictable thou art.
Why must thou torment a young woman's heart?
Why must you cause her anger and despair
When the washing line from its posts you tear?
Into the mud plunges a sheet,
A fresh pair of socks has muddy brown feet.
There are shirts in a tangle and towels in a mess
And whatever happened to that lacy, pink vest?

You gave the illusion of being so fine
But five minutes after the clothes are a-line,
You spit and you blow
You thunder and pour.
The wind is so strong
It slams the back door.
The clothes which were hung on the line to get dry
Are soaked by the deluge that floods from the sky.
And so, far from thinking her task has been done,
The poor lady finds she has hardly begun.

## BRIEF ENCOUNTER

A man
Just stepped
Into my life
And
Out
Again.

## HOMEWARD BOUND?

Cream topped
Denim skirted
High heeled
Short haired
Bag over shouldered
Girl
Where are you heading?

## STRING

*(How long is a piece of string?)*

String can be long -
As long as you want it.
Long enough to fly a kite
Long enough to tie you up tight
Long enough to wrap round a tree
Or to cast a fishing hook into the sea.
String can be long.

String can be short -
As short as you want it.
Short enough to tie in a knot
Short enough to mark the page you forgot
Short enough to tie up a shoe
Or to secure a parcel to Auntie Sue.
String can be short.

String can be as long or as short as you want it.
It can be long enough to roll into a ball
Or so short that it's hardly there at all.
String can be
As long…
Or as short…
As you want it.

## COMMUTING

Into the train again.
Jam-packed
Crammed
Clinging, swinging
Commuters
Bumping into one another
But looking away.

Strangers embracing
To the movement
Of the train
Look blank
As if nothing mattered.

But seemingly blank minds
Whirr with activity
Replaying the previous day
Planning the day ahead
Behind nothing-matters masks

They pour from the trains like lemmings.
Pushing and shoving,
Bustling and hurrying,
Bristling and struggling,
Faces strained as they pass the barrier,
A working day
A whole working day
Ahead.

## WATCHING THE SUN THROUGH A CLASSROOM WINDOW

Sun
Sinking sun
Sinking radiance in grey sky.

Cloud
Broken cloud
Broken cloud spliced by knife edge light.

Rain
Fallen rain
Fallen rain glistening in puddles.

Tree
Leaf lost tree
Leaf lost tree silhouetted against broken sky.

Sun
Sinking sun
Hitting grey horizon
Extinguished by falling rain
And
Gone.

# Portishead

## TIME PASSES FOR DREAMERS

We were young back then

In a time that seems

Not so long ago.

But to you it's time

Beyond time.

We were dreamers

Dreaming dreams.

Older now,

We are dreamers still.

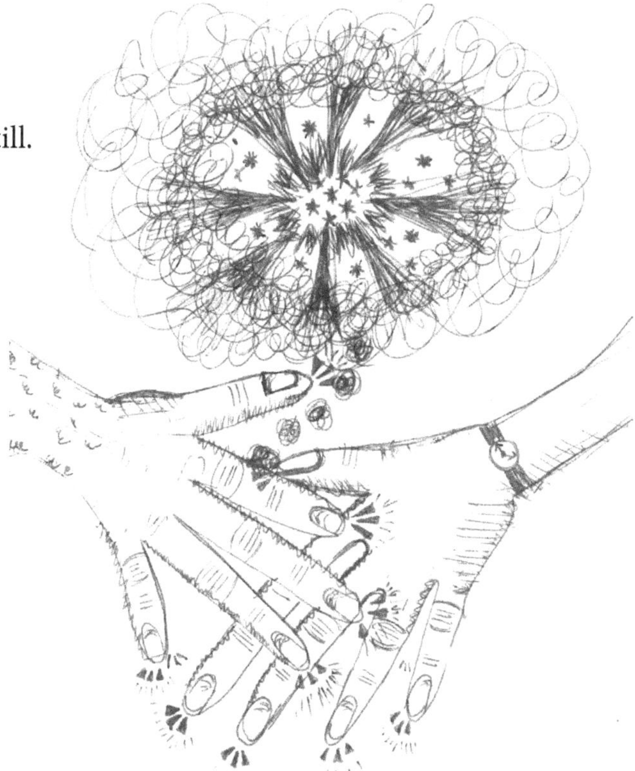

## RAIN

Rain
Falling
Dashing the sky
To dull grey.
Chilled air
Damp, soggy leaves squelching
Underfoot
As puddles settle
In the dimples
Of the ground.

Rain splashing bare legs
And dampening spirits
Smiles washed away
Drowned.
Gloom settling like a cloak
Over the September afternoon
Sunless and bleak.
No trace of summer remains.

But we can still dance
Still laugh
Still love
In the rain rinsed afternoon
We find ourselves in.

## ONLY AFTER THE RAIN

*(A poem built using Magnetic Poetry)*

Only after the rain
Eternity in a moment
After love
When sorrow descends
Hearts grow lonely
After love
Hearts grow cold
And time stands still
For those who weep.

What song did summer sing?
Weave words
Delicate and strong.

Man may ask for beauty in a woman
Though wisdom and compassion
Are better companions.

Beneath this moment
Beauty and love
Flood through
My cool, purple garden.

Soaring like a symphony of sweet music
Let a thousand whispers
Laugh like wind
Above the lengthy shadows.

# Life on Location

## SUNSHINE AND SHOWERS

The weather forecast,
And the weather.
As unpredictable
As Life.

It's not until you step outside
That you know what the weather holds
Just like life.
In your head
Dreams, plans, possibilities
Hopes and fears…
It's only when you step into them
That they become reality.

Showers and sunshine
Stepping into puddles…
And out again.

A gloomy day
And I'm gloomy.
The sun shines
And my spirit soars.

So, when it rains
Remember the sunshine
And hold on
To the rainbow.

## SPACE; NO SPACE

Stars, moons, planets
Whizzing through darkness
SPACE

Mountains, forests, heathland
A lonely road through miles of emptiness
SPACE

A crowded room
People pushing
Constantly demanding
My time, my attention,
My decisions
A busy, no-time-to-think day
NO SPACE

## SILENCE

*(Inspired by 'I Like that Stuff' by Adrian Mitchell)*

Phones ringing
Machines vibrating
Noise – I hear that stuff.

Hammers banging
Drills whirring
Noise – I hear that stuff.

Children shouting
Whistle blowing
Noise - I hear that stuff.

Music blaring
Cars racing
Noise – I can't get away from that stuff.

Someone's just invaded it
Hurled a shout into it
Silence - I need that stuff.

Can't get enough of it
Noise deprives me of it
Silence – I need that stuff.

How far is a place with it?
It's said God's best heard in it
Silence – I really need that stuff!

## FOG

Fog hung limply through the valley
Traipsing along the motorway
Lingering with uncertainty
As if it didn't really know
Why it was there.

Warning lights flashed,
'Fog. Fog. FOG!
Drive slowly –
No –
Slower than that.
Take care!
You can't see where you are going.'

And yet, up above
The sky was blue
The sun was shining.
It should have been
A beautiful day…

Is life sometimes like that?
From where we stand, it's
'Fog!
Take care!
You can't see where you are going!'

From God's viewpoint
Clear blue skies
Fog in patches
Down below.

If only we could see through the fog!

FOG
Action
Yes!
That way.
This way...
Thought
somewhere
Nowhere
Big choice
little choice
Decisions

# Hampshire

## RUINS

*(written in the Old Bishops' Palace, Wolvesley, Winchester)*

Stone walls stand majestic, proud and broken
Against the blue cloud-flitted sky.
Ruins deep seated in history,
Walls prayer soaked and silent.

For centuries people have sought God here
Sought Him and found Him;
Asked of Him and received from Him.
Resolve has been strengthened here,
Spiritual quests revitalised,
Faith journeys determined.

These ruins stand on ancient foundations,
As faith stands on ancient foundations;
Foundations laid before the dawning of time
As the WORD was spoken into DARKNESS,
'Let there be LIGHT!'

And the light has been there to dispel every darkness
Ever since.
LIGHT and LOVE
Celebrated in a baby, a child, a man
The man whose very being yielded light
The man who carried every sorrow, every sadness

To the place of Death.
And LIGHT conquered darkness.
Darkness never puts it out.
This is the truth
That these ruins proclaim.
Christ has died
Christ is risen
Christ shall come again.
Light in the darkness
From everlasting to everlasting.
Firm foundation.
No question.

## A WALK FROM KEYHAVEN

It was just a walk – one we'd done many times before
But never at that hour of the day
Just as the sun was beginning to set,
Its splendour colouring the sky
And the light of evening
Reflecting in the still waters of the lagoon.
Mist hovered over the meadows,
Wispy and ethereal
Geese honked in V-shaped formations
Traversing the sky
Before settling
On to the lake.
As they circled in formation,
A lone swan stretched out its wings
Measured its performance
And ascended majestically
Indulging in a brief turn of flight
Before plunging back
On to the surface of the lake.

And as darkness descended,
Peace and tranquillity
Wrapped themselves around the landscape,
Wild returning to the wild we were momentarily party to,
Before stepping back
Into the human domain.

## STILLNESS

In the stillness of the moment
The sun dancing on the rippling waves
Its warmth seeps
Into the million speculums of sand
Timeless
Still
Bluest blue sky
Over bluest blue sea
Captured
In a photo
Unchanging
Unmoving
Timeless
Still.

## PEACE OR CONFUSION

A white dove sits on the telephone wire outside
In peace and tranquillity
It sits
Silent and still.
But inside, just a few metres away,
A wasp frantically hurls itself at the perspex ceiling,
Unable to track a course to the open window.

In my world, everything seems peaceful
But news broadcasts report a fatal earthquake
In someone else's world.
Hundreds have died in Italy.
A region is devastated
Rescuers work tirelessly
Searching for survivors.
My quest to save a frustrated wasp
Seems futile in comparison.

Beauty destroyed
Life snuffed out
For travellers buried at a food festival.
Earthquake
Unpredicted
No tremor forecast
No rumblings expected

No final fond farewells made.
No-one expected the belly of the earth to spew out
Treacherously today.

For some, it changed everything.
Memento mori
Remember you are mortal.

## WINTER INTO SPRING

Against the grey rain-ladened sky
One denuded tree
Stretches its branches
Holds firm to its shape
Clutching to the cyclical certainty
That Spring follows Winter
And there is hope.
Its blueprint
Intrinsic
Life giving
Yearning for change
As its buds struggle to form.

## FINDING JOY

Joy used to be found at the end of a long drive

Which wended its way through the woods and over a bridge.
Joy used to be found in an old house,
Once part of an estate,
Set in a beautiful garden
Where bees hummed and birds cooed.
For fifty-nine years, Joy was found there.
And then, one day,
Quite inexplicably,
It tip-toed away.

Once Joy had left,
Staying was no longer an option.
The search began.
Needed: A new home
Wanted: New owners for the old house.

As the pieces slotted into place
Unwanted belongings were cleared away
Boxes were packed
For the move
To a new home
Which would open its doors
To offer warmth, safety, belonging.
The Finding of Joy.

# Yeovil

## WATCHING RUGBY

Grass flying through the air
Bodies bundling
Tree trunk legs flailing
Faces planted
Sweaty and grass splattered.
Energy electric
Crowd ecstatic.

From the moment of the battle cry,
The opposing team,
Standing firm
In battle horn formation
Accept the challenge delivered.
Purposeful and determined
With a title to hold on to
Or to snatch away.

Focus
Strain every sinew
Work together
With synchronised
Determination.

'The first job
Is to win the line out.'
And the second job?
The second job
Is to win the game.

## NAME GAME

Don't hurt Bert.
Don't call Gertie, 'Dirty'.
Don't hit Jed across the head!
Don't be mean to Jean.
Don't step on Pete's feet.
Don't stare at Claire.
Don't whack Jack.
Don't leave Elaine
Standing in the rain.

Instead,
Why don't you
Offer Jake a cake,
Give Fred a book you've read,
Let Mike ride your bike,
Play a game with Jane,
Take Mark to the park
And as for Tim,
Be friends with him.

## PINK HAIR

You are the lady with pink hair
You've had pink hair
Since before pink hair
Was a thing.
Your pink hair says,
'I am one of a kind
Unique, exciting, creative
Notice me.'

You are the girl with blue hair
Your blue hair catches my eye.
Blue hair says,
'Look at my blue hair
Don't look at me.
My blue hair is worth looking at
Just look at that – not me.'

You are the woman with red hair.
Red hair says,
'My hair was a dull brown.
Not interesting.
I needed a change
To say something.
To be different -
Not just one of the crowd.'

## Hair Today

Pink hair, blue hair, red hair,
Green hair, purple hair, silvery grey hair
Hair colours from packets, from jars from tubes
Peroxide blonde hair, glossy dyed brown hair
Black, black, black hair
Dyed at the salon
Or over the bath at home.

Why do they do it,
These dyed hair ones?
Are they afraid of getting old
Of being unnoticed,
Of being themselves?
Or are they just ready for a change?
Hair today,
And gone tomorrow?

mystery
BLUE
Pink
Red
Discount
Colour
+ Cut Salon

## MEANING – WHAT DOES IT MEAN?

We all spend our lives
Searching for it.
Elusive as shadows
Fragile as eggshells
Changeable as the weather
Multi-faceted as a rhomicosidodecahedron.
Dictionaries
Are crammed with it
Encyclopaedias and textbooks
Are stuffed with it
Google and Wikipedia
Depend on it
Museums
Are teeming with it
Philosophers' heads
Pulsate with it.

Theologians
Professors
Detectives
And Scientists
Devote
Years to it
And in the end
We're all

# Yeovil

Looking for it.
Who's hidden it?

Meaning
Significance
Value
Purpose
Was it all worthwhile?
Life?
What does it mean?

There are more questions
Than answers
Always something else
To understand.
Perhaps
In the end,
All you need
IS Love.

## HOME

'I'm going home.'
'She's gone home.'
'I want to go home.'
'When will we be home?'
'There's no-one at home tonight.'
Home.
The place we long for
A safe- haven
A place of peace.

What does it mean to be 'home'?
I've moved home so many times in my life
The homes that are no longer 'home'
Just become places
Where I once lived.

Is the place I live now
Home
Or just a place to come back to
When the day is done?

If I feel 'homesick' now,
Am I just longing for a time and a place
That no longer exist?
Where is my home?

What about those whose homes are not safe places?
Those who've lost their homes
In war, earthquake, or flood?
Those who've been thrown out, moved on?
Those who can only call a doorway
Or a sheet of cardboard on the street
Home?
Where is home for them,
The home-less?

What does home mean?

## TRAVEL OR AN EMPTY NEST

(for our daughter and sons.)

Travel
But come home.
Explore the world
But allow this country
To gently hold you
And draw you back.
Search out,
Quest and question,
Discover and discuss,
Be enriched
Stretched
Deepened,
Be set free.
But know,
Always know where you belong.
This country is your own
The nation in which you were born.
You are rooted here
By history.
Rooted, but free to wander the globe.
Travel
Travel…
But promise you'll come home.

PowerPaddle
N
S

## VISIT

We miss you
We've missed you
We're missing you
Then suddenly
You're here
Filling the space
With your presence
Your stories
Your smiles
Your enthusiasm,
Your energy
You're here
You're here
You're here
You're…gone again
And the space where you were
Is filled
With your absence.

## BACKWARDS AND FORWARDS

Only a humming bird
Can fly backwards.
Walk backwards,
Dance backwards,
But you can't live
Backwards.
Life moves only one way -
Forwards.

## FLYING LESSON

I am a bird
I have wings
I have wings so I can fly.
I am trying out my wings-
New wings
On a new bird-
Trying out my wings to see what they can do.

I'm fluttering
Hovering
Lifting up
Flapping at the wall
Trying to reach the top.

I'm fluttering
Hovering
Lifting up
Flapping at the wall
Sinking down.

Trying again
Fluttering
Flapping
But my wings
Aren't quite ready yet
Not for such high heights…

I'm flying
But not high…
I am a bird
Trying out
My new wings.

L

## A MOMENT IN TIME

Flickering, but unmoving,
The clock's second hand
Twitched and juddered -
The moment frozen in time.
Twenty to seven and forty seconds.
Still twenty to seven.
In this room,
Under this clock,
It will always be -
Twenty to seven
And forty seconds,
Whilst time
In the rest of the world
Moves on relentlessly
Second by second
Minute by minute
Hour by hour
Until, momentarily
Just for a second,
The time here coincides
With the rest of the world
Twice each day.
Time here stands still
Until someone finds a new battery
And allows it to move on.

## SOUNDTRACK

Films
Have a soundtrack.
Lights, camera, action,
Cue sound.
The story unfolds
As the music plays -
Films have a soundtrack.

Life
Has a soundtrack
The humming of traffic
The ticking of a clock
The buzzing of insects
The twittering of birds.
Children shrieking with delight as they play
Deafening roar as the crowd witness a goal.
Water splashing in the shower,
A kettle boiling,
The doorbell,
The ping or ring of a phone,
The crunch of tyres on the gravel.

Music
On the radio
On Spotify
A favourite CD

## Life on Location

Playing in the background.
Some people self-select a continuous soundtrack.
Constant music reverberates through their brains
Pumped in by headphones
Connected to their ears.
But even without music
Life has a soundtrack.

Life has a soundtrack
Words
Always words
Words spoken
Words heard
Words in a constant stream
Marching through my head
Thoughts
My 'always' soundtrack
Even when no-one else is there.

## TO BE...

To be or not to be
Is that really the question?
Surely 'to be' is the answer
We're human be-ings.

'Be the best you can be.'
How can I be that best
In a world that is so confusing?
A world set on fast forward
With everything rushing by,
Rushing by
Fast
Too fast for me
When I'm trying just
To be.

## LAUGHTER

Music.
Beautiful, resonant, restorative
Music.
Echoes of joy
Cascading, dancing,
Ricocheting, rippling.
People laughing
Sharing
Together
Community
Laughter.

## FRIENDSHIP

*'Let this be a timeless place where we can reflect upon the true value of friendship.'*

*(Quote on an art installation at Bucklers Mead Academy, Yeovil)*

A timeless place
A place untouched by time
A place where time stretches out
Reaching beyond the 'now'
Encompassing all that was
And all that is to be.
A timeless place
With the stillness
Peace
And rhythm
Of an endless caress
Of waves upon the shore.

And friendship?
What does it mean?
To 'reflect upon the true value of friendship'
Should we consider the value of individual friends
Or ponder the virtues of friendship as an abstract form?
What is it about friendship that the human soul craves?
Do we give ourselves time
To nurture it?

Friendship -
That need to connect with another
To be valued
And affirmed
Free to express ourselves as we are
No barriers
No pretending.
A place where we can be brave enough
To face our insecurities
Our inadequacies
Our failings
Without fear
Knowing that we will be accepted
As we are
A friend.

## FRIENDSHIP – 2

*'Let this be a timeless place where we can reflect upon the true value of friendship.'*

How many friendships are forged in a school?
Start of the Autumn Term
New pupil
New faces
A blur
No-one you recognise
No-one you know.
No-one who knows enough about you-
So, explain who you are.

The same questions
What's your name?
Where did you come from?
Where did you go to primary school?
How long have you been here?
Why did you come?

New lessons
New teachers
New classmates
New subjects
New timetable.

## Life on Location

Weeks pass
The timetable
Repeats
Repeats
Repeats
Familiar faces
In familiar rooms
At familiar tables

And soon from the blur of faces
Individuals emerge.
Individuals who share the same interests
The same joys and struggles
Individuals who share a joke,
A sandwich,
A pen.

And from that blur
Friendships begin to flower-
Some that will last a short time,
Some that will last for all of school,
Some that will last.
Last forever.

Friendship.

## WITH PASSING TIME, TIME PASSES_

Looking at me
You probably think
I am old.
I am not yet old,
Not nearly as old
As I hope to be.

Inside I am young,
Running free across the sand
Holding the string of a kite
Delighting in daisies,
Bouncing balls
And sunshine.
Inside I long to be creative
Spontaneous
Innovative
Inspirational
Energetic.
But gradually
I feel my energy ebbing,
My enthusiasm deflating,
Like a soggy helium balloon
Weeks after a party.

Let me treasure my memories.
Let my dreams hover,
Like dandelion seedlings
Caught up
On a summer breeze.
Let me still dance
Still laugh
Still bring joy
To the hearts of those I love.

I am neither young nor old
But still somewhere in between
In a place
I want to hold on to.
But I know it will slip away
Like sand through my fingers
Or water in a stream.
I cannot hold it
And soon this moment will be beyond my grasp.
Time.
The days stretch out, dangling their minutes before me.
But the weeks, months, years
Whizz by in a blink.

Hehe hehehe hehehe

## CORNER COTTAGE

Corner Cottage
No Parking

No parking
No barking
No larking about
Don't stop for a chat here
Don't laugh and don't shout.

You will not be welcome
Don't think you can stay.
'We'll put it more plainly –
Please go away!'

Your message is quite clear.
You do not want us here.
We will not park or bark or lark
We'll hurry on our way.

## FAST CAR

I side-step on to the verge.
Retreating from approaching cars
I stand at the lane's edge.

One car slows
Its driver waves

Another speeds up
As it goes passed
Fast.

Driver,
Are you not aware
That I am there
Or don't you care?

## THE APPLE PICKERS OR TIME FOR ANOTHER APPLE CAKE, MRS T.

Before the Autumn winds
Ravage the laden tree
And hurl its ripened fruit
Smash, splatter
On the ground below,
The apple pickers assemble.
A motley crew equipped
With ladder, calico sheet, and cardboard boxes
They meander into the garden,
Looking upwards and pointing
At the apples cowering between branches.

The ladder is positioned
It's A-frame stretched to the limit
And 'Ladder man' ascends its narrow rungs
Responding to cries of
'Back a bit'
'Just to your right'
'There's one by your elbow'
'Watch out for the rose bush.'
As sheet-stretchers
Stretch the unwieldly canvas,
Apples bounce and tumble
On the calico trampoline.

Apples sorted into boxes.
Those 'worthy of a produce show',
Are destined for Mrs T's apple crumble
Or delicious Dorset apple cake.

Another box for bruised and battered
'Sort today' apples
And a bucket for shrivelled, moulding
'Never make it into a pie' apples
For the compost.

They braved spiders,
Falling apples,
Stubborn branches,
Rose thorns
And with tools packed away,
They sit eating apple cake.
A job well done
And wasn't it fun?

# Pembrokeshire

## MANORBIER CASTLE

Tall, towering
Stones hewn
For permanence
You have stood
Longer
Far longer
Than those who hewed
Your stones.
They passed
Centuries ago
Whilst you stand proud,
Though in ruins,
Dominating the clifftop
And capturing my gaze.
Crows
(Or are they rooks?)
Make their nests among your ramparts
And smaller birds dart
In and out
Of your vacant windows
Just for fun.

# Manchester

Tram Day Saver
Tea
Sweets
Tobacco
Grocers

## A WEEKEND IN MANCHESTER

I thought you were
Unkempt
Run down
Dirty and chaotic.
But instead
I found you to be
Bustling
Well-organised
Vibrant
And innovative.

I thought you would be
Grey and gloomy
But you sparkled with lights.
Your trams whizzed me
From place to place
Affording me
Excellent views
Of the city
Whilst keeping me dry.

It rained constantly
As I spent the weekend
Under steel grey skies.
But that weekend
It rained everywhere
In this sodden country –
And Manchester,
I loved you.

## STRANGERS NO MORE

We entered the room
As strangers
But as we danced
In our own space,
Yet sharing the moment,
And as we partnered
And forged connections,
We became,
Not strangers,
But community.
We didn't know much
Of one another's story –
We didn't need to know.
We were there and we were
Accepted,
The experience of dancing,
Dancing, dancing
Connected and affirmed us.
For that time,
We belonged together.

## DANCING IN MANCHESTER

Music spilled into the hall
Spreading its notes,
Its rhythm, its pace,
Relentlessly across the floor.
Sounds ricocheted from the walls
Reverberating through
The spaces
Between us
Until each and every
One of us
Was bathed in its mystery
And compelled
To dance.

The music flowed through our limbs
Its changing energy
Pulsing
Staccato beats.
Chaos ensued
Jangling my thoughts,
Shaking my limbs,
Dismantling my equilibrium
Until it passed on
To lyrical
Movements that spiralled
And flowed and spun.
Rising and falling,
Energised and restored
Ready to receive
Stillness
And peace.

# Dumfries and Galloway

## FIRE CIRCLE

Embers in log pile
Encircled by hard, flat stones
And damp log stumps
Flickering flames
Fire.
We stand,
Nibbling nuts and
Drinking oak leaf wine,
As we wait
For the saucepans
To emerge from the van.
Dhal and vegetables
Seasoned to perfection,
Crusty, rustic bread.
Fruit salad –
An unusual mix.
Avocado, banana
Apple, melon, grapes
Raspberries.
Delicious and sweet.
As we eat
We play
'Ten Top Fruits'
Under the sky's fading light
And the fire crackles.

## MIST AND MIDGES

Coffee and café
A retreat from the rain
Postcards from the shop
And tickets for a play.
Rain easing
A short drive
To park
By the loch.
Walk
To the Bruce Stone.
Climb
Through the forest
Into the mist
Way above the midges
To reach the top.
Breath-taking views
'So glad we came…'
We talk of this and that
As we descend the steep track
Rain soaked but happy.
We race to escape
Those hungry, biting midges.
Leaping into the car,
With a slam of doors
We swat at those biters
Who dare to follow us.

# Spain

## BRIAN BILSTON DOESN'T DRIVE

You don't have to drive
To be a poet.
A car
Will get you far
But so will a train
Or a plane.
A plane?
I think I'll take a plane
To Spain.

## SPAIN

In the dark of night,
In the pouring rain,
We left a sodden England.
Taking flight
We headed to Spain.

## MALAGA TO ZAMORANOS
## THE M-Z OF DRIVING THROUGH OLIVE TREES

M
Malaga
Mountains
Piled up
One behind another.
Roundabouts
And roads
Leading in all directions.
Letters and numbers
Attempt to let me know
Where we should go.
On paper it looks fine
Just follow the line
Through names of places
Passed cars with no faces.
The numbers confuse me
The place names bemuse me
And the list of instructions
Make no sense
As I struggle to find
How the words on the page
Relate to the world
Beyond the window.

## Life on Location

I am the navigator.
The navigator navigates.
The navigator
Knows where to go
Gives clear instructions.
But I do not know where to go
And my instructions are not clear.
But we drive on,
As you get used
To going right
Around the roundabouts
Look left, drive right,
Keep on the right side,
Which seems all wrong.
Just like my instructions.

Mountains
Piled up
One behind another
Olive trees
Neatly in lines
Or planted haphazardly
Where olive stones fell
Centuries ago.
A castle on a hill
(Not the one Ed Sheeran sings about)
And Watch Towers
Built by African Moors.
White villages with long names
I can't pronounce

And finally
One that matches
The last on my list.
One I thought
We'd missed.
The road narrows
Then opens into the village.
Zamoranos
Zamoranos
Its silent houses
Shuttered for siesta
Its streets silent
And deserted.
'Down a steep hill,
Over a bridge
Turn left
Pass the ruined farmhouse'
Instructions I understand.

And it's there
Ahead of us.
The driver drove,
The navigator navigated.
Destination
Z.

## TAKING THE DOG FOR A WALK

Booted up
With route map in hand
We set off on 'Walk 1.'
The route will take us
From the hotel
Along the road
Through olive groves
Up dusty tracks
To the left of a pine forest
And along a ridge to a Moorish Watch Tower
For spectacular views.

The dog-
A brown and white
Bouncy variety
With stumpy tail
And boundless energy-
Appears to be following us.
We try to send him back
But with endearing persistence
He sticks to our track.
'It looks like we're taking the dog on our walk.'
Or is he taking us on his?
It seems after all
That he knows the way.

We stop to read directions
But he's one step ahead.

From time to time,
He wanders off
And we call his name
Worried that we might
Lose him.
But he's just seeking shade
In the heat of the day
And soon scampers back,
Tongue lolling.
We try unsuccessfully
To offer him water
But it falls wasted on the ground.
A little further on
He rests in the shade of the Watch Tower
To peruse the view
He's clearly seen before
Whilst we – amazed-
Take photo after photo
Capturing the spectacular panorama
From many angles.

Down the hill
Passed more olive trees
Along the road

Life on Location

Close by the river
And we think we've lost him.
Before long, he returns
Dripping and thirst quenched
Having taken a river dip.

We're on the homeward stretch
With the hotel back in view
And he bounds off
Job done.
'Look we're back.
I've taken the people for a walk
And I didn't lose them.'

## ON THE TERRACE

Overlooking the pool
With olive-tree covered hills
Rising and falling
Behind it,
The terrace
Is an ideal place
For guests
To eat dinner
On this warm,
Late autumn evening.

The wooden slatted tables
Glimmer
With light from the bulbs
Set deep and low
Along the wall
And lanterns flicker
Bathing the table
In a warm glow.
Delicious food
Lovingly prepared,
Carefully plated,
Courteously delivered
Appreciatively savoured.
'Thank you very much,'
'That was so tasty.'
And the cicadas sing
In the darkness beyond
As a few twinkling stars
Peer out
Dancing on their nightly walk
Across the heavens.

# Yorkshire

## ON ILKLA MOOR BAHT'AT

Ilkley Moor without a hat?
Bonkers!
Rain freezes on your coat
Ears freeze inside your hat
Frozen fingers cower inside gloves
Wind whistles round you
And through you
Chilled to the bone.
Keep moving.
It's warmer that way.

Cow and Calf Rocks above
Cow and Calf pub below.
We ascend
And climbing through the rocks,
A foot jams,
Locked in a rock vice.
Take off the boot –
It's the only way out.
The wind whistles round you and through you.
Chilled to the bone, keep moving.
It's warmer that way.

Slipping and sliding
Across slate slabs

## Life on Location

Traversing squelchy bog
The path wends uphill
And there they are.
Twelve Apostles
Standing in a stone circle
For century after century after century
They hunch
Stone-deaf and silent.

Nestled in a wall,
A poem box
Playing to its stone seat auditorium,
And waiting for walkers
To pause
To write or read
Poems left in its care.
But chilled to the bone,
We keep moving,
Descending to the other Cow and Calf -
It's warmer that way.

POETRY

# New Zealand

## ARRIVAL

I've come so far
And lost a day
(Where did it go?)
Now I've arrived
On the other side of the world.
How does it feel to be
Half a world away
From the place I call home
And the people I know?

Right now
It's hard to say.
I'm sitting drinking coffee
In an airport
That could be anywhere.
Anywhere at all.
Same McDonalds
Wagamama Noodle stand
And Tork hand-driers
As back home.
Same sparrows…
Same sky.
It's time
To step outside.

## A POET IN NEW ZEALAND

'No job now'
Doesn't seem
Like the right thing to say
When asked from your occupation
On an immigration form.

So
I pause
Pen poised…
'Poet'
I write
As I step into this land
Which is
In itself
A poem.
Its land, its people, its words
Poetic.
And being a poet here
Seems just the right thing
To be.

## JET LEG

Travelling by plane
Around the world
Tumbles you through time
Messes with your mind.
The rhythm of
Wake, eat, work, eat,
Work, walk, eat, relax,
Sleep
Has been shaken
Out of place.
The meals we were given -
Dinner, breakfast
Dinner, breakfast -
Made sense
In terms of
Flight routine
But where was I?
Which time?
On which day?
I tried to sleep
When the lights went out
When my eyes grew heavy
But was I really ready?
Guess I didn't sleep much
Hunched up in my seat

## Life on Location

A sleep of sorts,
But not complete.
And now I'm home
In which time zone?
My disorientated head
Feels heavy
My worn out limbs
Heavy
My eyelids
Heavy
I force myself
To keep them open

But
Unwittingly
They're down.
I shake myself awake.
It's still day
Keep going
Keep going…
Keep flowing, growing
Why do I feel so strange?
It must be jet leg
I mean jet lag.

Words begin on my lips
But hang forgotten

I've lost their endings
Somewhere
In this shift of time
Am I losing my mind?
I try to sleep
(The clock says I should)
Sleep, sleep deep
Weird dreams
Colliding in my head
Making no sense.
(Are the prices here in dollars or pounds?)
Sleep, wake, no sleep
Sleep, sleep deep, no, wake.

Sleep
Awake
No. I ought to be in bed.
My head is filled with clouds and fog.
I'm saying the words
But it feels - unreal
Going through the motions
I've crossed over
Two oceans.
I try to
Sleep, wake, eat, work,
Eat, work, walk, eat, relax, sleep.
But somewhere

## Life on Location

Things aren't happening
In quite the right places.
I'm sorry if I don't seem
Quite myself.
I think I've got jet leg
I mean jet lug.
(It's been going on for days)
So just for now
Be patient
When it takes me too long
To get out my purse
To pay
And my mind is converting
The price to dollars.
I want to put on suncream
When I need a woolly hat
I'm cold
Then too hot
My stomach feels
Hungry
No, sick.
Am I sick?
No, tired.
And I wonder
How do they do it?
The pilots
And cabin staff

Who are repeatedly
Crossing time zones?
Time in turmoil
Day and night
Night and day
Day and day
Muddled
With snatches of sleep.
How do they survive?
Their lives must be
One long
Jet leg.

?!?
TIME ZO-NE 4
T-I-M-E Z-ON-E 1
TIME ZONE 2
T-IME Z-O-N-E 18
TIME